Window
ADVENTURE™

VENUS
The Morning Star

CLAUDIA ALEXANDER, PhD
PLANETARY SCIENTIST
BOOK 2

STEM Science Learning

Windows to Adventure™: Book 2 Venus, The Morning Star
A product of:
Red Phoenix Books
www.redphoenixbooks.com

Publisher's Cataloging-in-Publication Data

Alexander, Claudia.
    Windows to adventure: Venus, the morning star / Claudia Alexander.
    p. cm.
    ISBN 978-1-937781-19-4 (e-book, fixed format)
    ISBN 978-1-937781-21-7 (e-book, dynamic format)
    ISBN 978-1-937781-22-4 (pbk.)
    ISBN 978-1-937781-36-1 (Hardcover)
    "Science Learning, Book 2"
    Summary : With help from a magical creature named AboGado, Rashad and Angie visit planet Venus and explore the surface
    Includes bibliographical references and index.

1. Venus (Planet) --Juvenile literature. 2. Venus (Planet) --Exploration --Juvenile literature. 3. Solar system --Juvenile literature. I. Title.

QB621 .A44 2014
523.4/2 --dc23

BISAC Subject Headings:
JUVENILE NONFICTION / Science & Nature / Astronomy
JUVENILE FICTION / Fairy Tales & Folklore / Cultural & Ethnic
SCIENCE / Earth Sciences / Geology
TECHNOLOGY & ENGINERING / Aeronautics and Astronautics
NATURE / Sky Observation

Illustrators:
Terry Lim Diefenbach (cut-paper)
Jennifer Kindert (characters)
Joe LeMonnier (maps)
Gary McKluskey (assorted)
Eli Ziv (assorted)

Book Layout: Opus 1 Design www.opus1design.com

Astrophotography credits: see end of book

Edition: 1

Red Phoenix Books

CONTENTS

Foreword

Building the Magellan spacecraft to visit Venus was challenging work. We needed inspiration. I used to go outside every night and look at Venus in the sky. I used to imagine being there, and imagined the spacecraft flying through the sky. Day after day, building the spacecraft, we used the sight of Venus as our inspiration. One day maybe you'll be inspired to go outside and look at Venus too!

Tony Spear
Manager of NASA's
Magellan Mission to Venus

Chapter 1
Rashad's Room

"AboGado, you said we could visit planets." Rashad's words spilled eagerly into the air. He sat on the floor in his room addressing what looked like a worn out picture frame. His friend, Angie Coradini, the girl from next door, sat beside him.

Nothing happened. For a split second, Rashad's spirits sank. "How are you supposed to make it work?" he wondered aloud. He looked at Angie who shrugged.

Rashad Johnson pronounced his name "Raw-shod." He liked to call Angie "Pigtails" just to see how steamed she could get. He did it now. "You're the smart one, Pigtails, figure it out."

Beside him, Angie actually growled. Rashad grinned. He knew she was getting ready to call him "Rush-odd," the way his mother sometimes did. Rashad admired Angie for being so smart, but he didn't feel like he could tell her straight out. He and Angie had found AboGado together in the old orchard across the street from where their two houses sat.

Angie brought it home in her backpack, but he knew they both wanted an excuse to bring it out again.

"What did we do last time?"

"You kicked it, remember?"

"Oh yeah," Rashad was embarrassed. "It looked just like an old piece of wood." He reached out to prop it up against his bed. "Maybe it has to be sitting up."

How would he ever prove to his friend Julio that the thing worked? Julio would laugh him off the playground. A talking window? Rashad felt sick.

Then, in slow motion, the little object sprouted arms, hands, legs, and feet. It opened its shutters. Eyes appeared at the top of the window frame, spaced wide apart! It swung its tiny legs over its head, and then sprang into an upright position!

It had grown to the size of an artist's easel. The window was dark, just like it was the first time they'd seen it. Its apple-sized eyes and wider mouth looked friendly but frozen, as if they had simply stopped moving smack in the middle of a sentence.

"Ahh!" Rashad scrambled to get away.

Chapter 2
Questions for AboGado

"**Y**ou were awake the whole time!" Rashad accused.

"You can't just expect me to spring into action at the snap of your fingers," AboGado snapped his wooden digits for emphasis.

"We want to visit Venus," cried Rashad eagerly. He remembered the lady in the billowing yellow dress from

their last adventure. She had invited them to visit anytime they wanted. Well, they wanted to visit now!

AboGado frowned sternly and shook a finger at Rashad before closing his shutters and folding his arms. "You have to ask the right questions for the magic to work!" He paced back and forth in front of

them, as if waiting for a perfect response.

"Oh," Rashad glanced at Angie. He wasn't sure if he should ask about the mysterious lady. AboGado didn't seem to be in the best mood.

Pigtails looked like she was thinking and not paying attention to Rashad at all.

"What does the planet Venus look like?" Angie asked, changing the subject.

"Good one," said Rashad. He had to give it to her. Pigtails always came up with good questions. "But can we go to the real Venus? Through the window, I mean."

"Will it be safe?" added Angie.

"It will if I protect you," warned the AboGado.

"But I wanted to feel what it was really like to be there!" Rashad could hear his own voice climbing high, and he cleared his throat to bring it back down to normal.

"You can't go there without protection," said AboGado. "It's too hot, and there is not enough oxygen to breathe. So you can't really feel what it is like on the surface. It's not safe for you. You need to be in an environment like the one you have on Earth. You'll have to wear the bubbles."

"Not again!" Rashad turned away. In their last journey, AboGado made them wear bubble suits to visit Mars and Venus. It said the suits were for protection, but the suits felt like being inside a plastic bounce house he'd played in once at Julio's birthday party—completely isolated from the grass and stones in Julio's backyard. He wanted to get outside and feel it for real, not just pretend.

When he was alive, Rashad's father was a fireman of distinction who wore two black stripes on his helmet. Mr. Johnson had experienced real danger and real risk all the time. Rashad wanted nothing more than to prove that he was as brave as his father, not reckless, not "Rush-odd" as his mom always called him.

Venus

This photo shows the surface of the planet Venus. Venus is always covered with clouds, so views of the surface, like these, come from the Magellan mission (which could see beneath the clouds). This picture has been colored a special way to show different elevations. Low elevations are shown in brown, and higher elevations are shown in yellow. The light yellow in the middle shows the region called Aphrodite Terra. This is one of three regions that most closely resemble Earth's continents

Chapter 3
Venus

While they were talking a figure approached in AboGado's open shutters. It was a woman, floating toward them.

"But if you *really* want to feel what it's like on Venus…" AboGado was saying.

"Yes, please," said Rashad. "Can we?"

"Is that her?" interrupted Angie, pointing.

"Hello," said the lady. "I represent a planet that bears the name of the Roman goddess Venus, the goddess of love. You can call me Venus, if you like."

Everything about her was yellow. She had light yellow skin the color of a pear, and dark yellow eyes. Long, thick red-yellow hair flowed behind in billows past her knees. A thin dress flowed as she floated, as if a gentle wind was moving with her all the time.

Venus waved a hand and the night sky appeared before them as if she'd painted it with a paintbrush. A pleasant red glow colored the horizon.

Venus
in small bright phase

Moon

Suddenly Rashad realized that he wasn't in his room anymore, but outside on the grass.

"I am the Morning Star."

Venus pointed to the sky above. Rashad could see a very bright star burst into the sky above the glow of the horizon.

"I am the second planet from the Sun, after our brother Mercury, who is closest to the Sun, and before our sister Earth, who is third from the Sun."

Venus explained, "Because I am so close to the Sun, I can be seen from Earth at only two times of day: in the evening as the Sun is setting, or in the morning before the Sun rises. That is why I am called both the Morning Star and the Evening Star.

Venus
in large faint phase

"If you wish to find me in the sky," she continued, "look toward the Sun at sunset, that's when you can see me best. I look like a star. Only the Moon is brighter.

"Other times I am not so bright. You can barely see me. That is one way that you can tell that I go around the Sun. If you looked at me every night for a year, you'd see me get brighter and then dimmer. That's because I am sometimes close to you on Earth and other times far away."

"I've never seen you before," said Angie.

"You probably have seen me, but didn't know it. Next time you'll know it's me," Venus smiled.

"Because I'm always seen so close to sunrise or sunset, people thought I had something to do with the Sun, like making it move, getting it out of bed and ready for the day, or putting it to bed at night."

17

The Phases of Venus

As planet Venus orbits the Sun, it appears to change size and shape. As shown in this series of photographs from 2002, when it comes closer to the Earth, an observer from the ground sees it go from a "full" phase to a "crescent" phase.

Venus, Morning Star
in Motion Past the Moon

This 2012 time-lapse photograph, lasting nine minutes, shows (a) the relative motion of Venus compared to the Moon as (b) Venus and the Sun rise in the sky. It is the Earth that's turning while the Moon is relatively still! Venus can be seen at first below the Moon, then moving behind the Moon, and after about six minutes, rising beyond and above the Moon's position.

19

Map of the Toltec Nation

The Toltec people lived in central Mexico. The orange oval in the upper map shows where their territory once was.

Venus Legend

A Tale about Venus
from the Toltec

To the Toltec people...

The Morning Star's job
was to...

...make the Sun go!

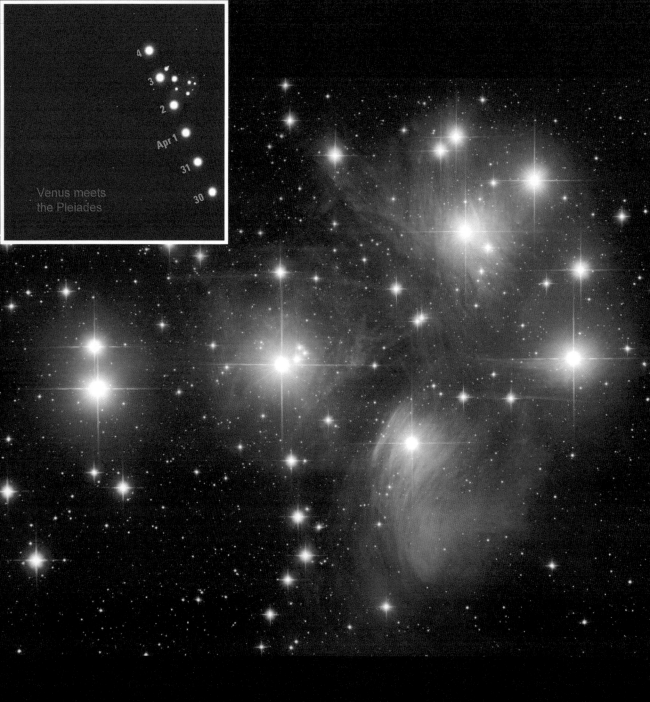

Venus meets
the Pleiades

These beautiful stars are called *the Pleiades.*

They are a small part of the constellation known as Taurus the Bull. They form the "shoulder" of the bull.

The inset shows Venus moving past the Pleiades on March 30– April 4, 2012.

The Pleiades

"Like the other planets, I am a wandering star," she continued.

"What does that mean?" Rashad couldn't believe they were back in his room, and the lady was inside the window again.

"It means that I don't stay in place, year after year, with the same neighbors every night for eternity.

Venus pointed out the window of Rashad's room to the sky outside, "If you looked at me night after night, you would see me against a background of stars. You would notice that I move among them and have new friends every month.

"For example," she said, "in 1996, I was near the constellation Taurus from April to August. Then I moved on to visit the constellation Gemini.

"In 1997," Venus smiled, "I visited fifteen different constellations."

What's a constellation?

A **picture** in the sky made out of stars is a **constellation**. What is more, there are lots of names for these pictures.

This is the **constellation Cassiopeia**, the big "W," (or "M.")

Can you find Cassiopeia in this photo?

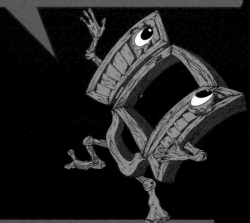

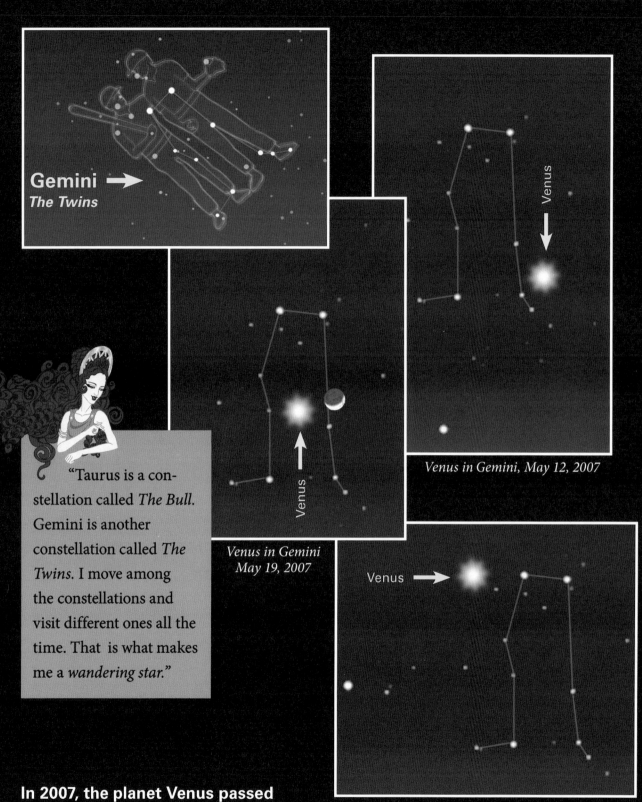

Gemini →
The Twins

"Taurus is a con-
stellation called *The Bull*.
Gemini is another
constellation called *The
Twins*. I move among
the constellations and
visit different ones all the
time. That is what makes
me a *wandering star*."

Venus in Gemini, May 12, 2007

*Venus in Gemini
May 19, 2007*

Venus →

Venus in Gemini, June 3, 2007

In 2007, the planet Venus passed
through the constellation of Gemini
in May and June.

Chapter 5
Through the Window

"**W**ould you like AboGado to take you there?" asked Venus.

"Can we? Please!" Rashad jumped up, hitting the floor of his room hard when he came down, all the while looking into AboGado's large metal eyes.

"When do we start wearing our bubble suits?" asked Angie.

"Just as soon as you step through," said AboGado.

AboGado's frame grew large and wide before the kids" eyes until his tiny legs completely disappeared. Soon his edges reached the ceiling of Rashad's room and stretched from his closet on one side to the trophy case on the other side where his Little League trophies were perched.

The Temperature on Venus is 863° Fahrenheit 460° Celsius

Rashad gulped. Dad would go through, he thought. He clambered over the sill right onto the cloud! The footing felt squishy, but he felt triumphant.

Angie was right behind him. Just as AboGado said, her whole body was encased in a clear bubble suit. Rashad held his hand up. Sure enough, it was encased too.

Rashad looked back through the window and saw his bed and comic book collection in his room right where he left them.

Then he looked around. They were riding on a giant cloud-thing, with temple-like columns made of rotating clouds. The columns that held up the ceiling looked like nothing so much as miniature tornadoes. He looked down over the edge of the cloud and saw that the ground was a long way away. They were traveling faster than an airplane flies. "Whoa!" Rashad shouted.

"Welcome to my cloud cabana," said Venus. She pointed at two cloud stools she had made for them. "Sit here."

"Careful where you sit," came AboGado's voice from a distance.

Angie jumped up. "Is it safe?" she asked Venus.

"Of course, perfectly safe," she replied vaguely.

"AboGado said Venus is too hot," said Rashad, positioning himself on the strangely unstable seat that moved on the air as if on waves in the sea.

Rashad tried hard to peer past the clouds to see the action on the ground.

"What's the hottest day you can imagine?" Venus asked Rashad, seating herself on her own, more elaborate cloud couch.

"100 degrees," answered Rashad without hesitation.

"Well, it's a lot hotter here," said Venus with a smile. "It's almost 900 degrees, and the day is only beginning! Earth has it so easy. She can make it rain. It is a tough job getting it to rain here. I've tried and tried. It is so hot that rain evaporates before it hits the ground."

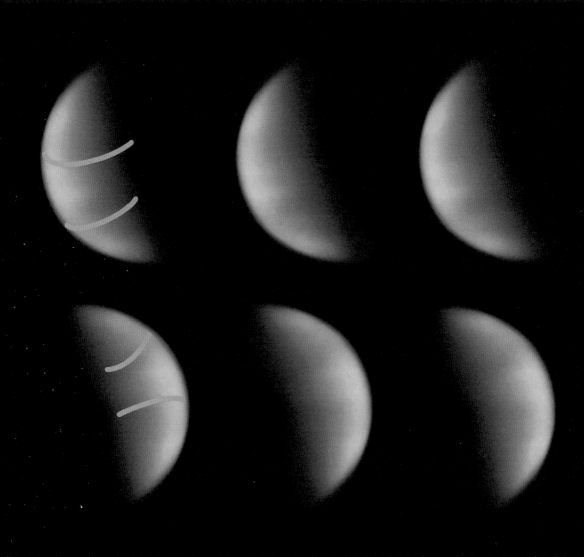

The clouds of Venus

Venus is completely covered with clouds. It takes special equipment to see under the clouds. These photographs show the classic sideways "V" pattern that is a persistent pattern in Venus's atmosphere.

Outer space

Sulfuric acid clouds

50KM

Sulfuric acid and dust

Troposphere

Venus's cloud cabana flies just below the clouds.

Chapter 6
Riding the Super-Rotating Wind

"People from Earth have given me many different jobs," Venus laughed. "According to most legends, as Morning Star, I prepared for the coming of the day. Sometimes I would scatter the red glow of early morning around the sky to show that day was coming. Other times I cleaned up after the Sun, sweeping up the stray light

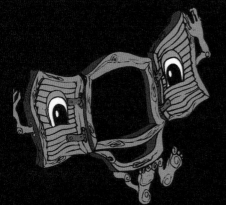

Venus rotates backward compared to any other planet in the solar system

EARTH
Global winds blow
this way at 160 mph

Earth spins
this way at
1000 mph

VENUS
Global winds blow
this way at 260 mph

Venus spins
this way at
4 mph

leftover after sunset. In another tale, I had the power to speed up the coming of day. It wasn't easy. Sometimes I needed some convincing," she said with a wink.

Rashad was trying both to pay attention and also look over the side beyond the yellow-white clouds below them, toward the rapidly moving ground he could see far underneath. He felt someone tugging on his bubble suit. It was Angie.

"Be careful!" said Angie. "It is a long way down."

"How high up are we?" asked Rashad.

"We are about fifty kilometers up," said Venus. "That's about thirty-five miles."

"Thirty-five miles!" Rashad wasn't sure how high that was, but it sure sounded like a big number. "Is that higher than an airplane flies?"

"About five times as high," Venus answered.

"Why is the ground moving so fast?" Angie was peering below now too.

"My super-rotating wind is propelling us forward at a great speed," Venus replied.

Super-rotating wind. It reminded Rashad of the time he went to Chicago on the train with his mom — smooth with the occasional bump.

"Wow," said Rashad, "I wish I could feel the super-rotating wind without the bubble suit!" Rashad turned to look for AboGado but they'd already moved far away from the little window with the opening to his room.

"Are those mountains?" cried Angie.

Rashad turned so quickly to see that he fell off of his wobbly cloud stool, and onto his knees on the soft floor of the traveling cloud cabana. It was as soft as a giant feather bed. Rashad crawled over to Angie to check the view.

"We are at Aphrodite Terra," Venus announced, "the biggest land mass on the surface of the planet."

Ishtar Terra

Aphrodite Terra

Lada Terra

The Surface of Venus

The surface of Venus as seen by the Magellan mission. It's the same as the picture on page 14, only on this page it's enhanced to show different elevations in blue (lowest), green (medium), and pink (high). The three regions that most closely resemble Earth's continents are labeled.

Chapter 7
The Face of Venus

"I have three major land masses," said Venus, coming over to look at the ground with them. "They can't really be called continents, because unlike Earth, planet Venus has no ocean to separate them. So they are called highlands."

She pointed to the vast area of high ground beneath them. "The biggest of them is called Aphrodite Terra, named after the Greek goddess of love."

Western-most part of Aphrodite Terra
In this perspective view, taken from the Magellan spacecraft, the highlands (right) are colored blue, and the lowlands (left) are colored red and orange.

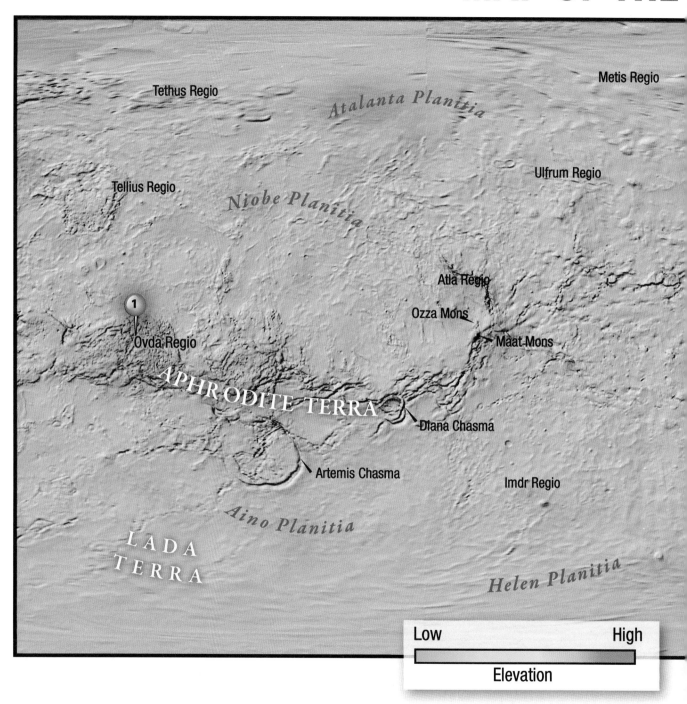

Tethus Regio

Metis Regio

Atalanta Planitia

Tellius Regio

Ulfrum Regio

Niobe Planitia

Atla Regio

Ozza Mons

Maat Mons

Ovda Regio

APHRODITE TERRA

Diana Chasma

Artemis Chasma

Imdr Regio

Aino Planitia

LADA
TERRA

Helen Planitia

Low	High

Elevation

SURFACE OF VENUS

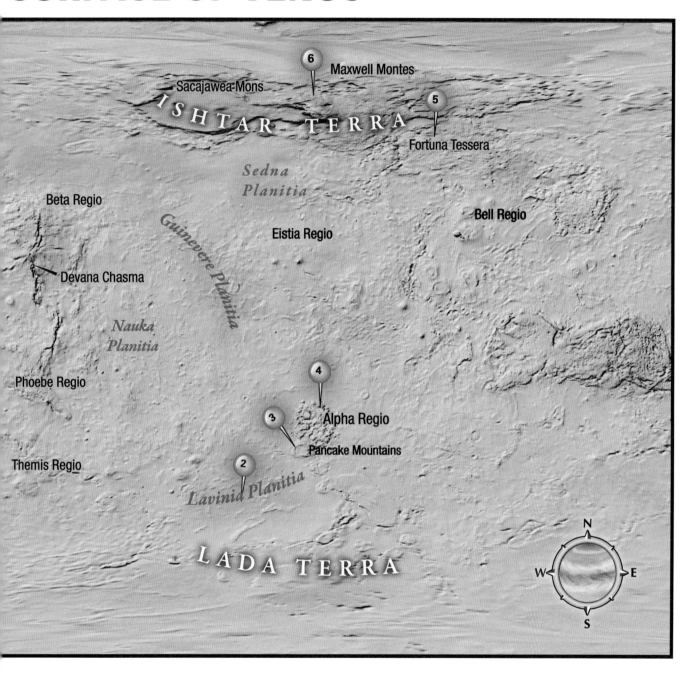

Maxwell Montes

6

Sacajawea Mons

ISHTAR TERRA

5

Fortuna Tessera

Sedna
Planitia

Beta Regio

Bell Regio

Guinevere Planitia

Eistia Regio

Devana Chasma

Nauka
Planitia

Phoebe Regio

4

Alpha Regio

3

Pancake Mountains

Themis Regio

2

Lavinia Planitia

LADA TERRA

N

W   E

S

"We are going to visit the north pole, the south pole, and the equatorial region of Venus on this tour. We'll start here at the western edge of Aphrodite Terra, at a place called Ovda Regio."

Even Rashad could tell that the ground at this place was much higher than the surrounding territory beneath.

"What happened to the ocean?" demanded Rashad. "Did all the water evaporate?"

"There is no ocean," said Venus solemnly. That's why there are only highlands and lowlands. The highlands resemble Earth's continents, but continents made of continental crust are quite different. The lowlands resemble Earth's ocean basins, but oceanic crust is much different."

"Where are the other highlands?" asked Angie.

Rashad noticed that Angie stopped stressing so much about safety. She must be enjoying this trip like it was the school carnival to let her guard down, he thought.

Venus pointed toward the north pole. "Ishtar Terra is the next largest. Ishtar is named after the goddess of love from the ancient people known as Babylonians." She pointed toward the south pole, "And Lada Terra is third, named after the goddess of love from an ancient people known as the Slavs."

"I see a river!" Rashad turned to find Venus beside him. "Is that a river down there? There is water!"

"It's a channel, all right," Venus leaned out as far as she could.

"There's no water down there," said Angie, who seemed to be staring as hard as Rashad was, but she was not close to leaning as far off of the cloud cabana as was Venus. "Don't you see how hot it is?" Angie demanded. "How can there be water?"

Rashad raised his hand to his face. He didn't feel anything but comfortable inside his bubble suit By the shimmering of the atmosphere Rashad could finally distinguish waves of heat billowing up from the surface.

Venus has neither oceans nor official "continents."

Venus does have HIGHLANDS and LOWLANDS. Highlands resemble continents. Lowlands resemble deep ocean trenches.

The three major Highlands are: Ishtar Terra, Aphrodite Terra, and Lada Terra. The four minor Highlands are: Alpha Regio, Beta Regio, Ovid Regio, and Theta Regio.

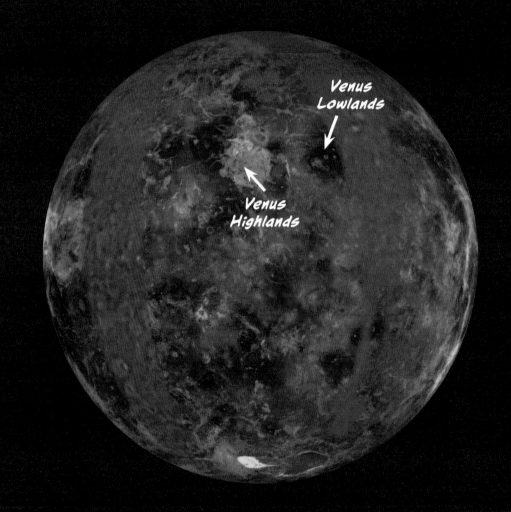

Venus Lowlands

Venus Highlands

Earth has both CONTINENTS and OCEANS.

A continent is a very large LANDMASS on Earth
that rises above the ocean. Continental "crust"
(the rocks of which it is composed) is distinctly
different from ocean "crust."

The seven continents are: Africa, Antarctica,
Asia, Australia, Europe, North America, and
South America.

North American
Continent

Atlantic Ocean

South
American
Continent

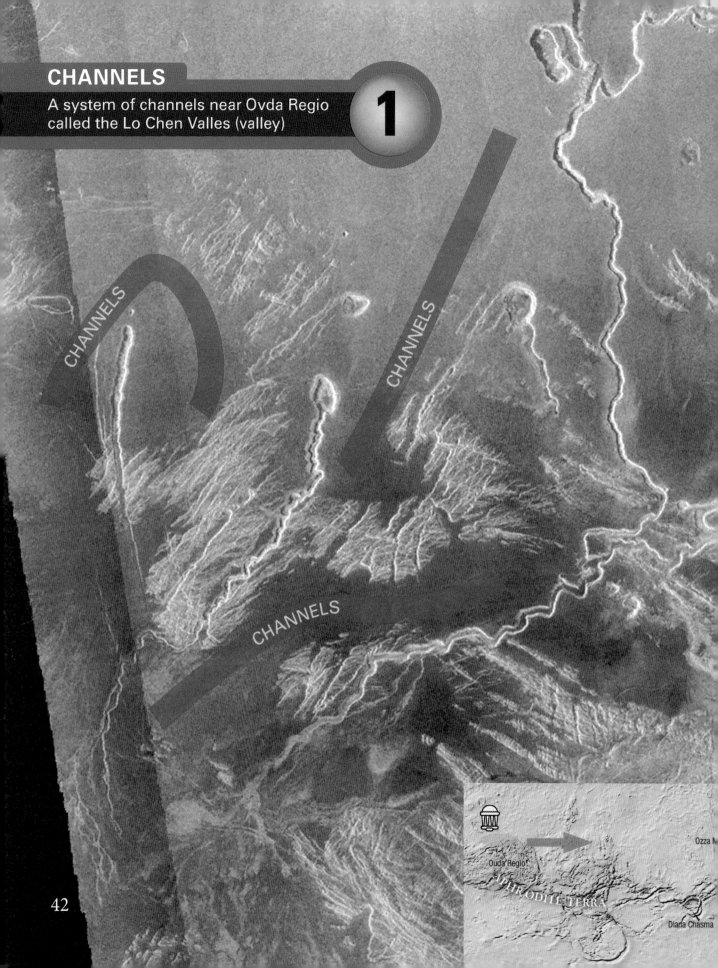

CHANNELS

A system of channels near Ovda Regio called the Lo Chen Valles (valley)

1

CHANNELS

CHANNELS

CHANNELS

Ouda Regio

Ozza M

APHRODITE TERRA

Diana Chasma

"Channels like these can be filled with material other than water." Venus pointed to the surface below. "That one was created by lava. See how it has a different color. You can tell because they get narrower downstream instead of bigger. Water systems on Earth go from small streams to large rivers to mighty rivers.

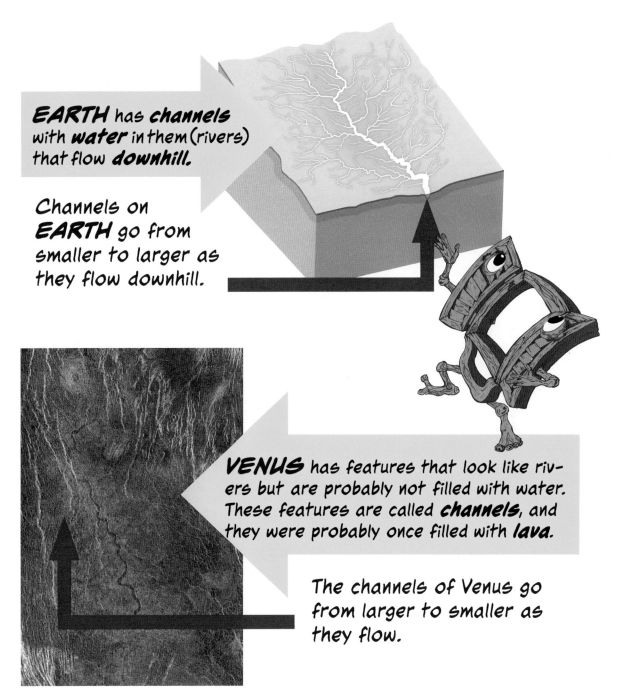

EARTH has **channels** with **water** in them (rivers) that flow **downhill.**

Channels on **EARTH** go from smaller to larger as they flow downhill.

VENUS has features that look like rivers but are probably not filled with water. These features are called **channels**, and they were probably once filled with **lava.**

The channels of Venus go from larger to smaller as they flow.

IMPACT CRATERS

Three examples of impact craters in Venus's southern hemisphere (near Lavinia Planitia).

2

Each of these three is 20 times the size of Earth's Meteor Crater in Arizona

Aglaonice Crater

Danilova Crater

Howe Crater

Alpha Regio

Lavinia Planitia

LADA TERRA

An **Impact Crater** is created when a **meteor** flys from outer space and hits (impacts) a planet with so much **force** that it makes a large **hole** (crater) in the surface of that planet.

Meteor Crater, also known as Barringer Crater

Meteor Crater, also known as Barringer Crater, in Arizona, USA. It's the largest crater in the United States, about 1,200 meters (about 12 hundred skateboards) in diameter, 170 meters (1.5 football fields) deep and is surrounded by a rim that rises 45 meters (150 basketball shoes stacked heel to toe) above the surrounding plains.

Most of the surface features of Venus are named after women

"Now we are headed south toward Lada Terra," Venus announced, with the official-sounding voice of a train conductor. She took a seat on her long cloud couch.

"Most of the features on the surface of Venus are named after women, sometimes legendary women like Helen of Troy, or Guinevere of King Arthur's court."

"Named after girls?" Rashad couldn't believe it. Pigtails would love that. Sure enough, Angie had a huge smile on her face.

Venus continued. "For example, the craters below us are named after a lady dancer, a lady poet, and a lady astronomer."

Rashad leaned over to see what Venus was referring to. Three giant holes in the ground unfurled below him. Each of them was bigger than any stadium he'd ever seen. Much bigger than Tiger Stadium in Detroit.

"Now we go north again."

"Bye, Helen Planitia," said Angie, waving.

PANCAKE MOUNTAINS

Pancake mountains, or "volcanic domes" are found all over Venus.

3

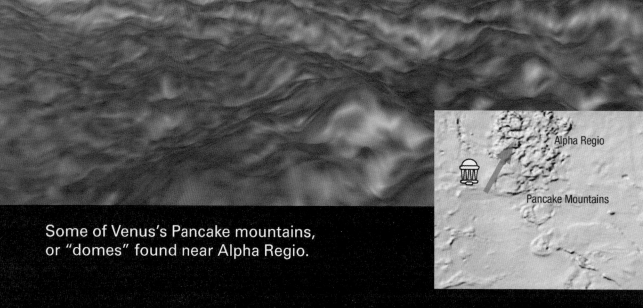

Some of Venus's Pancake mountains, or "domes" found near Alpha Regio.

Alpha Regio

Pancake Mountains

"This is Alpha Regio," Venus announced. "Alpha means "first." Alpha Regio was one of the first land masses scientists learned about on Venus."

Rashad could see a sharp difference between the plains in the distance, and the territory immediately beneath them. The ground rose abruptly higher, with steep cliffs marking the change. The rounded top and steep edges made this part of the surface look almost like a giant, flat muffin.

"Are there more mountains?" asked Angie.

"Of course!" came a chorus of new female voices from the surface below.

Girls" voices! Rashad peered over the side.

"Look there," Venus pointed to the edge of Alpha Regio. "There are some of my famous flat-topped mountains."

Rashad leaned forward to watch as the surface moved rapidly below them. The ground below them rose higher than that near the pancake mountains, but also looked folded up like an accordion on its side. "What's that?"

Volcanic dome in Arizona

"Volcanic domes are found on Earth all right, but they don't look **like pancakes**, as they do on Venus. Shown here is a little cinder cone, also called a "lava dome" or a "volcanic dome," in Arizona. They are **mini-volcanoes**, and the lava that comes out is thinner than that from a normal volcano. Venus's domes are about ten times bigger than the ones on Earth, and the cones on Venus seem to have collapsed under their own weight."

47

VOLCANIC RISES

A large "island" called Alpha Regio
is about the size of Mexico.

4

Alpha Reggio

Examples of Venus Pancake Mountains

Some land masses on Venus (Alpha & Beta Regio) formed over a permanent hot spot deep in Venus's mantle. The hot spot caused a portion of the crust to rise, like a loaf of bread in the oven. Lava flowed out, forming large **rises** known as **Volcanic Rises**.

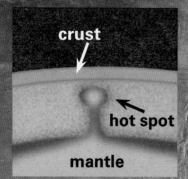

crust

hot spot

mantle

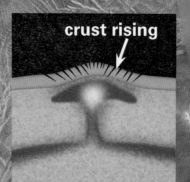

crust rising

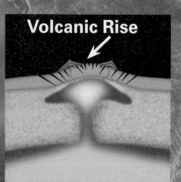

Volcanic Rise

Examples of Venus Tessera
(folded surface)

Alpha Regio

49

TESSERA (COMPRESSION)

Unlike Earth, Venus's surface has no plates. But the crust of Venus seems to buckle and fold like a giant rug.

Maxwell Montes

I S H T A R   T E R R A

Fortuna Tessera

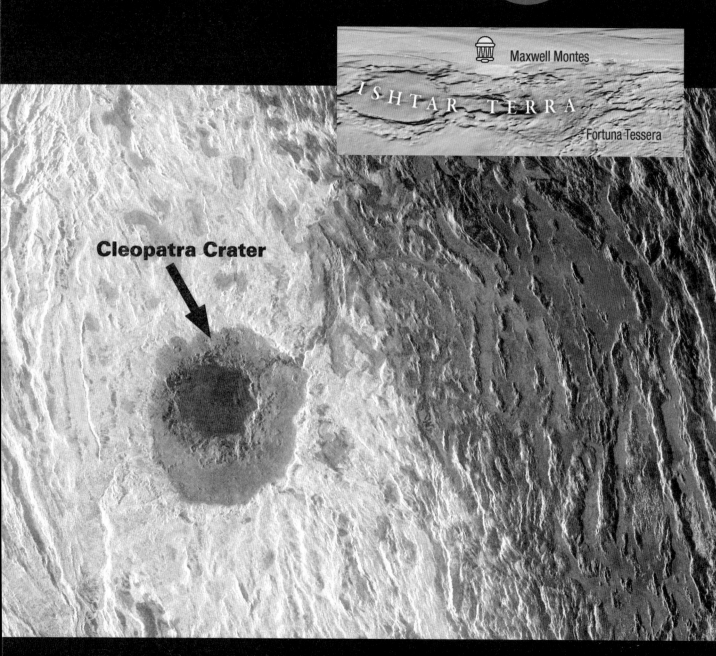

Cleopatra Crater

This picture shows the beautiful Cleopatra Crater found on the sloping side of Maxwell Montes (below left, out of the picture—see photograph on page 53). Cleopatra Crater was created in the middle of a tessera feature known as Fortuna Tessera (the dark gray folded region to the right).

"These rolling plains are called tessera."

"Tessa…What?" Rashad wasn't sure that was a word. He had never heard anyone say a word like that before, anyway.

Venus leaned back on her couch, and their entire cloud cabana seemed to pick up speed. Wind whipped past Rashad's face, pressing the bubble suit against his cheeks.

"We are going to the north pole now," Venus was almost shouting to be heard above the wind, "to see the best tessera."

"Tessa…What?" Rashad turned to the resident know-it-all, and raised one eyebrow, but Angie shrugged, looking uncertain.

"Look down," Venus commanded. She pointed, and Rashad turned to look.

"These plains are called Fortuna Tessera. Let's go down for a closer look."

Venus waved her arm, causing the cabana to whirl and spin. Rashad clumsily searched for something to hang on to, but his hand went right through the clouds. Angie was also struggling to stay onboard.

"We're falling out!" squealed Angie.

Venus calmly grasped each of them by the arm and sat them back down. "In the middle of these rolling plains is the great crater, Cleopatra. My biggest mountain lies farther to the east on the edge of the plains."

Venus has tessera

See how the **crust**, (surface), of Venus seems to stretch and fold like a wrinkled **giant rug?** This is called, **Tessera.**

Mountain ranges, rift valleys, and plate tectonics are evidence that Earth's surface is in motion

"If you were to take someone on a tour of Earth, what would you show them?" Venus leaned forward to ask each of them. "Would you show them the biggest mountains? Would you show them the biggest cities? What would you say are Earth's most important features?"

"I'd show…" Rashad's voice trailed off. He suddenly wasn't sure what would he show someone visiting Earth from outer space.

"Well," began Angie, "it'd be water, wouldn't it? Because, most of the surface of Earth is covered with water."

"Oh yeah," said Rashad. He imagined giant waves crashing over ships, like in the movies.

Venus leaned back on her cloud couch again, and a sly smile crossed her face. "There's something else. Evidence the surface of the Earth is moving."

"Mountains!" cried Angie. Her eyes opened wide with understanding.

"Not any one mountain," said Venus. "When a map shows mountain after mountain, adjacent to valley after valley, as if they were alternating piano keys, pressed by giant fingers. Well then, that map is evidence of a surface that folds and stretches. Geologists call it *compression & extension.*

Tessera are evidence that Venus's surface may be in motion

"The surface of Venus doesn't have plates. However, the surface of Venus shows evidence that the crust compresses and stretches like rubber.

"These rolling plains, called tessera, the most common feature of the surface, exhibit that very sort of evidence!" Venus exclaimed.

MAXWELL MONTES
A Mountain of Venus
Formed by Compression

The Steep Side

Maxwell Montes is the tallest mountain on Venus. In this picture, the peak is to the right where the color changes from dark gray to silver. Cleopatra Crater (from page 50) is out of this picture to the top right.

53

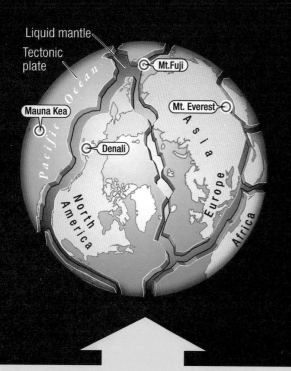

Liquid mantle
Tectonic plate

Pacific Ocean

Mt. Fuji
Mauna Kea
Denali
Mt. Everest

North America
Asia
Europe
Africa

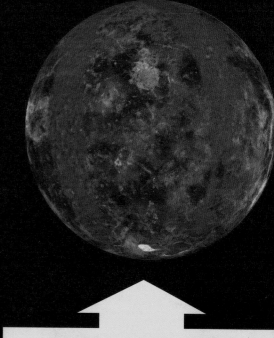

EARTH CRUSTAL PLATES

The Earth is broken up into huge, thick **plates** that drift atop the soft, underlying mantle, like film on top of a cup of hot chocolate.

Movement of the Earth's plates explains earthquakes, volcanoes, oceanic trenches, mountain range formation, and other geologic puzzles.

VENUS CRUSTAL PLATE

Venus is made up of only **one** crustal plate, but unlike the solid ridged tectonic **plates** on Earth, the plate on Venus is **bendable**, forming wrinkled plains, (tessera), and mountains (mons).

I wish our dinner plates could move themselves!

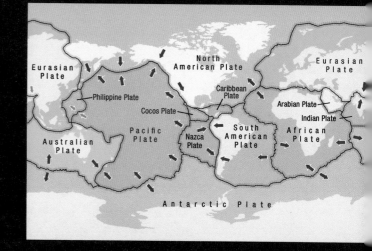

Eurasian Plate
North American Plate
Eurasian Plate
Philippine Plate
Caribbean Plate
Arabian Plate
Cocos Plate
Indian Plate
Pacific Plate
Nazca Plate
South American Plate
African Plate
Australian Plate
Antarctic Plate

Continents ride on top of these **plates** like a surfer on a wave!

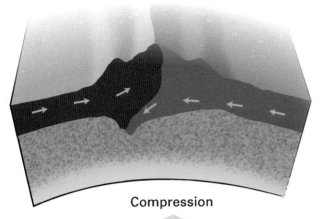

Compression

Let's take a closer look at crustal movements on Earth and Venus

COMPRESSION
(CRUSTAL SHORTENING)

When two plates **collide**, if both are too thick to be forced under the other, the crust is compressed, folded, and pushed **upward**. On Earth, the process can create mountain ranges.

Parts the surface of Venus form folded **tessera** and mountains. This is likely due to the same process, called compression.

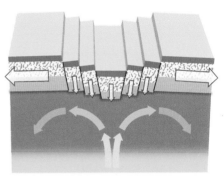

Rift Valley Formed by Extension

Extension

EXTENSION
(CRUSTAL LENGTHENING)

On Earth, forces can also pull the crust apart, just like a loaf of bread can be ripped **apart** by pulling at both ends. The crust of Venus does stretch, causing the surface to **sink** in places. This is likely due to the same process as that on Earth, called extension.

RIFT VALLEY

A rift valley is a deep **trough** in the earth, where a tectonic plate **splits** down the middle (by **extension**). A valley forms on the part of the land that was stretched.

Rifts (Crustal Stretching) on Venus

The Somerville Crater (round feature in the middle) in Beta Regio is split in half by a rift valley (dark gray feature).

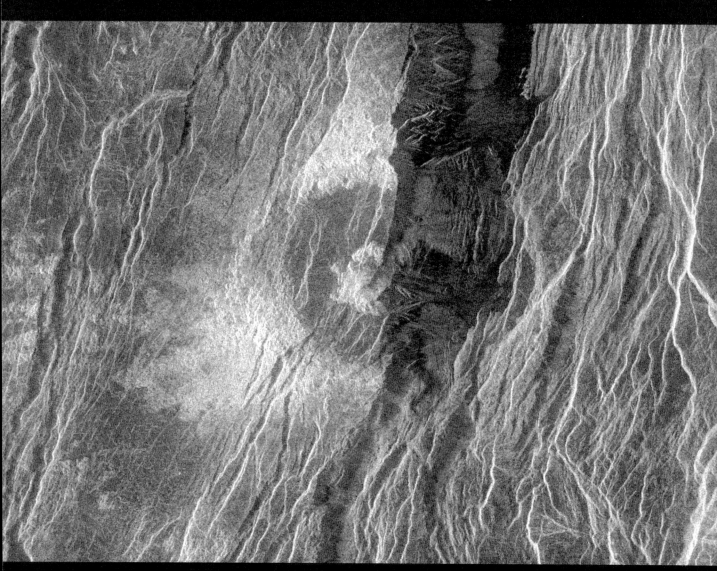

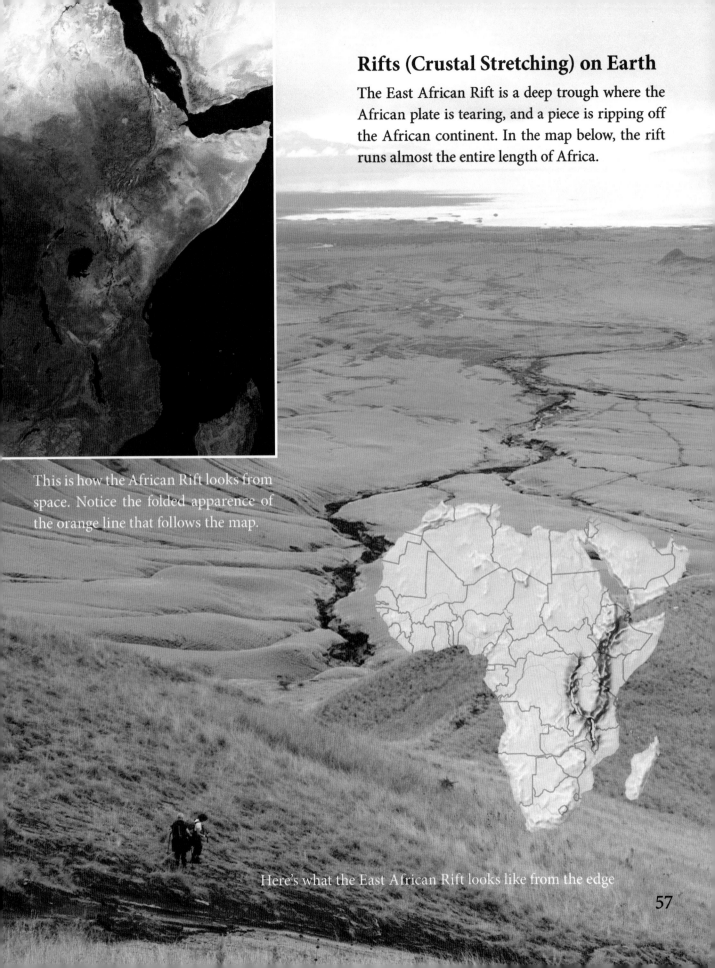

Rifts (Crustal Stretching) on Earth

The East African Rift is a deep trough where the African plate is tearing, and a piece is ripping off the African continent. In the map below, the rift runs almost the entire length of Africa.

This is how the African Rift looks from space. Notice the folded apparence of the orange line that follows the map.

Here's what the East African Rift looks like from the edge

Maxwell Montes is Venus's biggest mountain, part of a mountain range with the same name

Rashad looked down again. The rolling plains looked rather like the wavy surface of an old-fashioned long beard leading up to a chin. Suddenly, the largest peak in the mountain range took on a human face!

Beside him, Angie gasped. "It's him!"

Rashad recognized him too. The face belonged to Maxwell, the mountain they'd visited before. Venus positioned herself beside them to look over the edge of the cloud at the surface.

"That's Maxwell Montes, my biggest mountain range," said Venus. "Let's swing around and see it at closer."

Out of nowhere, the cloud cabana hit some turbulence. "Whoa!" shouted Rashad as he reached for something to hold onto.

He couldn't stop watching the action below. The side of the mountain range facing them was very steep, like a huge cliff! As they swung around they could see that the other side sloped gently toward the rolling plain. This was the one called Furtuna Tessera.

"Maxwell," Venus said, "is named after James Clerk Maxwell, who discovered of the mathematical relationships that explain light!"

"You came back," the voice of the mountain rumbled from below. Its eyes followed them as they circled in the air, and its mouth seemed to crinkle into a smile. "You can't come to Venus without visiting me." He almost preened with pride. "You don't see the likes of me anywhere else on this planet."

They were moving very fast. Soon the mountain range receded over the horizon. Rashad, Angie and Venus waved good-bye to Maxwell as they sped away. "Good-bye, Maxwell," called Angie.

Read more about Maxwell Montes in Book 1

Read more about different kinds of light, and the electromagnetic spectrum, in Books 6 &10

The Steep Side

The Sloping Side

Maxwell Montes
A mountain on Venus formed by compression

Milky Way Galaxy

Hyades Cluster of the
Taurus Constellation

The Pleiades

Moon

Venus

Jupiter

Venus over the Grand Canyon

This 2012 photograph of the Moon, Venus & Jupiter over the Grand Canyon also shows the Pleiades, the "V" shaped Hyades cluster, of the Taurus constellation, and the Milky Way (upper right corner).

60

Chapter 8
The Morning Star

"We are really moving fast," said Rashad. The wrinkled ridges and craters on the surface below seemed to blur.

With Venus motioning them to take a seat, Rashad turned his attention to their open-air cloud carriage. What Venus called her cloud cabana.

The ceiling overhead swayed and rustled with each turbulent bump, causing his cloud stool to shake. Columns of clouds, that twisted and tilted like tornadoes, barely managed to hold the ceiling aloft. Rashad glanced at Angie. She watched the ceiling too, as it tiled and swayed. He smiled at her, and she smiled widely back at him, nervously hoping their cloud vehicle was steady enough to last.

He spied Angie's backpack in the farthest corner of the cloud cabana.

"You brought your backpack?" Rashad whispered to Angie.

Angie shrugged.

Venus sat down next to them, plucked a tuft from the cloud and shaped it into a book.

"While we're passing over Guinevere Planitia, let's enjoy a story. This one is from the Seneca Nation—a people who once lived near New York."

Venus pretended to read the book, but Rashad noticed that she never once looked at its fluffy pages. It was her big smile that gave it away, he decided.

"The Seneca thought of the Morning Star as a male being," she said.

"Oh good," said Rashad. "Not a girl this time."

"Once upon a time, there was a boy," Venus nodded in Rashad's direction, "who made friends with the Morning Star..."

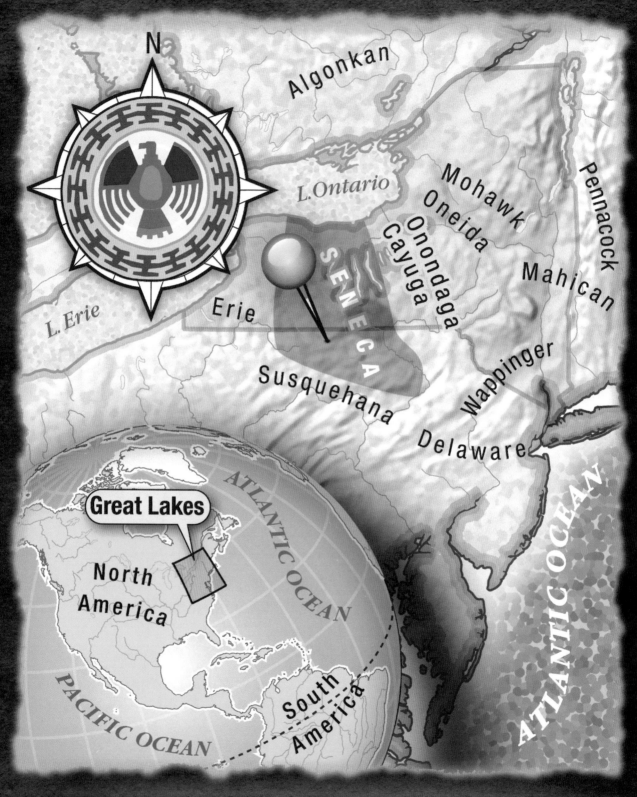

Map of the Seneca Nation

The Seneca people lived in North America in New York State. The green area in the upper map shows where their territory once was.

Venus Legend

A Tale about Venus from the Seneca Nation

"The Morning Star promised the boy that if he ever were in danger, he would help him," Venus said proudly.

"The boy grew into a skillful hunter. He was so skillful that the other young men in the village, even the son of the chief, were jealous," she went on. "He never worried about danger.

"But one day he got into trouble. On an island near their home, honey bees made especially good honey. The honey was delicious and bears guarded the bees carefully. The young man decided to try to gather some of the honey for the village, and he was successful. At the end of the day, he had filled a sack with honey. But he didn't notice the clever bear waiting for him to emerge from the hive.

"The bear chased him into a tree. The boy stared long and hard at the bear, waiting for it to go away. The bear paced and waited. The boy climbed higher in the tree. Night came and the bear still waited."

"Finally the young man took his eyes off the bear long enough to notice water marks on the tree. Nearby trees had similar marks, all at the same height — a height far over his head, and into thin branches where he could not climb.

"Hmmm, the young man thought to himself. This means when the tide rises in the morning, it submerges the trees. I'm in more trouble than I thought. If I wait long enough for the bear to go away, I'll be trapped by the rising tide.

"Hours passed, and under the moonlit night, the water began rising. When it reached a height taller than the bear could reach, the bear swam away, glaring at the young man all the while. The young man grew worried. He might have to call his friend, the Morning Star!" Venus raised her eyebrows to look at both of them expectantly.

"The Morning Star was attending to his duties, charging the Sun's cell phone, putting papers into his briefcase, and in other ways preparing for the Sun to commence his work. The young man called the Morning Star's name and the Morning Star looked down at Earth."

"The Sun has a cell phone?"

Venus laughed and continued reading.

"'Help me, Morning Star!" the young man cried. "I am in trouble." The Morning Star laughed then said, "I can see that.

"The young man waved one hand at the rising tide that was becoming a problem. "If you could make the day come quickly, then the tide will end, the water will go away, and I can return home.'"

"'Hold on!'

With that, the Morning Star retrieved the Sun, and brought the day. The waters went back to normal, and the young man was able to bring honey home to the village."

"Wow! I want a friend like the Morning Star. Nothing would be too difficult!"

Venus ·

Moon

Morning Star over Switzerland

Venus is the "Morning Star" in this photograph of the Moon & rising Sun over Switzerland.

Venus

Moon

Evening Star over Portgual

Venus is the "Evening Star" in this photograph of the Moon & the setting
Sun over Portugal.

Chapter 9
The Lord of Dawn

"Wow, I can't believe you were a man in that legend," said Angie.

"That's how the story goes," said Venus, standing up again. "According to the Seneca Nation, the embodiment of the Morning Star was a man. I appear however people want me to be.

"For example, to the ancient Mayan people of Central America, the Morning Star was a male god whose appearance was associated with war. When the Morning Star appeared in the sky, people were so afraid that they plugged their chimneys and windows so that the light would not enter their homes."

"Why war?" Angie sat on her cloud stool with one hand to her chin.

"The Morning Star was an enemy of the Sun and fought to take some of its light. His appearance meant the ground dried up, and humans would have to fight each other for corn.

"The Aztec people who lived in Mexico, neighbors of the Mayans, saw Venus as a peacemaker! As a mediator!"

"How can Venus be a mediator?" snorted Rashad. Seriously?

Venus looked toward where the Sun was positioned in the sky. "Day was the new world." She looked in the opposite direction, where the sky was already turning dark. "Night was the old world, or the Underworld." Venus looked again toward the Sun high in the sky, and pointed her whole hand in its direction. "The Sun was the Lord of Day, but had to travel through the Land of Night to return to his starting place every morning."

"To the Aztecs, the Morning Star was a prince known as the Lord of Dawn!" Venus stood and made a sweeping motion with one arm. "The Morning Star pushed the old world away and gave its place to the new world. As peacemaker and mediator, I was responsible for seeing that neither world encroached upon the other.

NEW SPAIN

Chichimecas

Tarascan

Otomi

Teponec

Totanac

Tenochtitlan

Tlaxcalan

AZTEC EMPIRE

Yopi

Mixtec

Maya

Zoque

Chiappan

Zapotec

Tehuantepec

Atlantic Ocean

North America

Mexico

Pacific

South America

PACIFIC OCEAN

Map of the Aztec Empire

*The Aztec people lived in Central America. The orange region
in the upper map shows where their territory once was.*

Venus Legend

A Tale about Venus from the Aztecs

Morning
Star

Sun

The Morning Star made sure the Sun was ready for work.

"Time to rise and shine, buddy, I have to announce you!"

The Morning Star's name was Quetzalcoatl (pronounced: Ket-zal-co-attle). His symbol was the winged serpent (dragon). He was the Lord of Dawn and had the power to go between worlds (day and night).

Evening
Star

Morning
Star

The Morning Star had an evil twin—the Evening Star! His name was Xolotl (pronounced: Shiol-ottle).

"Don't I know you from somewhere?"

The Evening Star had a dog's head for a face, and his skin was covered with smelly boils.

Evening
Star

Sun

The Evening Star greeted the Sun at the end of the day to escort him through the Land of Night:

"Did you think it was time for bed?"

The Evening Star was a prince of the Land of Night, and he could safely see that the Sun completed his journey.

"To the Aztecs, the Evening Star was the mirror image of the Morning Star and was a Prince of Night," she continued. "Where the Morning Star was a powerful mediator between old and new, the Evening Star was a terrible decaying god covered with boils and sores, who escorted the Sun during his travels through the Land of Night.

"Was he truly evil?" asked Angie, her hand still on her chin.

"The Aztecs believed that in Earth's earliest days, to help the human world, the Morning Star teamed up with his twin, the Evening Star, to steal fire from the Land of Night." Venus winked at Angie. "He always successfully escorted the Sun through the Land of Night. In that land, the Sun was never kidnapped by its ruler, the Lord of Night. So, in spite of how he looked, the Evening Star did good things."

Venus sat down again. "In a completely different part of the world, in ancient Greece, I wasn't a Lord of Dawn at all. Venus was a beautiful woman, a goddess of love, complete with powerful magic arrows that compelled people to fall in love!"

"I still don't understand how you can be a man and then a woman," said Angie. "How can you be a god of war, a god of peace, and a goddess of love, all in one Morning Star?"

"Oh! I get it," said Rashad. "Don't you see? Ooops!" He reached out as the cabana hit another bump and wobbled. "You see Venus in the sky," he fumbled for words, "this powerful, bright object, like a beacon, and it can embody different things to different people depending on where you live."

He'd never pass up a chance to see Venus in the sky now. "It's a strong presence in the sky, like the North Star." He thought of something else. "If stars were like a baseball team, Venus, a wandering star, would bat in the cleanup position. The most powerful on the team!"

Map of Ancient Greece

Ancient Greece was land of powerful cities.
This map shows where those cities were/are located.

Venus Legend

A Tale about Venus from Ancient Greece

A wood nymph named Echo, who can only speak when spoken to, falls for vain Narcissus

When she expresses her devotion, Narcissus is shocked!

Venus shoots arrows that cause those they strike to fall in love, and Narcissus falls for the first face that he sees—his own!

In time, unable to reach his true love, Narcissus turns into a flower, and by his side Echo fades into just a voice.

Chapter 12
Acid Rain

From the corner of his eye, Rashad could see his room approaching through the AboGado's open window. Their visit was about over.

"Good bye," said Rashad.

"Thank you!" called Angie.

Having stepped through the window into Rashad's room, Angie and Rashad turned to look at AboGado. The magical creature was shrinking back to its medium size. Its portal was already dark.

"Let's see how well your pants held up against the acid in the clouds," said AboGado, waddling over to look at Rashad's backside.

"Acid?" cried Rashad in alarm. He twisted himself around to see.

"Sure," said AboGado. "Venus's clouds are made of drops of acid. Much more acid than the clouds of Earth."

"No way," said Rashad. "Earth doesn't have acid clouds!"

"Haven't you ever heard of acid rain?" said AboGado. "There's a little bit of acid or base in every raindrop on Earth or on Venus. It's not a big deal. The rain on Venus is just a lot more acidic."

"Did I get it on me?" Angie and Rashad spoke at the same time, both looking at their arms.

"No, only on Rashad," teased the AboGado. "You'll know in a couple of minutes. There will be holes all over your pants."

"Holes!" cried Rashad. "My mom will kill me! You didn't tell me this would happen!"

"Going through the window is never without risk, young man," the AboGado scolded, leaning toward Rashad and standing a little taller.

"You said you would protect me," continued Rashad, his eyes a little wider than before.

"I did," said the AboGado. "You could breathe, couldn't you? You didn't fry in the heat, did you?" His hand waved back and forth.

"How come Angie didn't get acid on her?" asked Rashad. Angie was laughing at him.

"I thought you wanted to experience Venus for real," answered AboGado.

"Oh, no!" said Rashad with his hand to his face. "That's not what I meant."

"Be careful what you ask for," replied the AboGado, shrinking down to picture frame size again, "Especially when inside the world of the window."

The End

This book series is only the starting point for questions. To read more about any science topic presented in this story visit:

Windows to the Universe
www.windows2universe.org/

Sample Question: Is Venus a rocky planet or a gas planet?

Words We Used in this Book!

Acid - a type of liquid that is capable of dissolving or corroding a solid material on which it rests.

Channels - a stream carved into the ground; but on Venus, streams are created most likely by flowing lava.

Compression & Extension - see Extension; Compression is the part of the process in which a continent or land mass collides with, or is pressed against, another in a way that causes it to fold and buckle.

Constellation - a way that stars can be "connected" (like connecting the dots) to create a shape (or a letter) in the night sky.

Corona - half-moon shaped features on the surface of Venus that resemble subduction zones of Earth (see Subduction Zone).

Craters - a hole created when an object from space crashes onto the surface of a planet.

Extension & Compression - see Compression; Extension is the part of the process in which a continent or land mass is stretched in a way that opens ridges in the surface material

Domes - on Earth, volcanic domes are rounded hills (see Hill) underneath which lava is slowing making its way toward the surface. On Earth, seen from above, a dome might expand like bread rising in the oven to provide clues about the presence of hot lava close to the surface beneath. A dome will often stay frozen in place, even after the heat of the lava has subsided. The domes of Venus, another word for the so-called pancake mountains, formed because of a similar process of rising hot lava that never erupted, leaving a raised, circular, hill-like feature, that looks like a pancake when seen from above. These can be ten to one hundred times the size of volcanic domes on Earth.

Highlands - similar to Earth's continents.

Hill - the difference between a hill and a mountain? It is simply one of height. A hill is to a mountain the way a bonsai garden (miniature) is to a regular garden.

Lowlands - similar to Earth's ocean basins. (see Planitia).

Mons - is the word for mountain that applies to objects in space.

Montes - is the word for mountain range that applies to objects in space.

Pancake Mountains - an unusual sort of volcanic formation (see Domes), like a volcano, created by rising lava, but without the tall cones that area formed by Earth's shield volcanoes or stratovolcanoes.

Planitia - the word for flat plains. Applies to the lowland regions of Venus.

Quetzalcoatl (pronounced: Ket-zal-co-attle) - the Aztec name for the Morning Star

Rift - the word for a long, narrow, valley caused by the break up of the surface, in which, over time, the floor of the valley has fallen tens of thousands of feet below the original surface level.

Subduction (Subduction Zone) - the word for the process where one edge of a geologic plate, such as those found on Earth, is forced beneath the edge of another plate. A subduction zone is the place on the surface, usually accompanied by families of earthquakes, and nearby volcanoes, where that sinking process is happening. So far, no subduction zones have been positively identified on Venus.

Super-rotating Wind - a wind that blows faster than the planet rotates. Very unusual among objects in space, a super-rotating wind implies that there's a source of energy that's forcing the wind to go faster.

Troposphere - the lowest part of the atmospheric family. The layer of the atmosphere that is closest to the ground, with the most powerful winds. On Earth, the tropophere is the smallest member of the atmospheric family. On Venus, the troposphere is tall, stretching well over 70 km containing thick clouds, and super-rotating wind.

Xolotl (pronounced: Shiol-ottle) - the Aztec name for the Evening Star.

ABOUT THE AUTHOR

Claudia Alexander, Ph.D, studies the planets and flies spacecraft by day at NASA's Jet Propulsion Laboratory. By night she enters a fantasy world and reimagines the universe. Dr. Alexander enjoys the science of the Venus ionosphere (part of the Venus atmospheric family) and ways in which Venus behaves like a comet. Dr. Alexander studies comets, the thin atmospheres surrounding icy moons such as Jupiter's moon, Ganymede, and more recently, the way in which the whole protosolar nebula collapsed to form the planets.

She's served as Project Manager on the historic Galileo mission to Jupiter, and as the Project Staff Scientist on the Cassini mission to Saturn. She currently serves as Project Scientist on the NASA contribution to the European Space Agencies' Rosetta Mission, whose principal goal is to study the origin of comets by landing on comet 67P/Churyumov-Gerasimenko. Rosetta will ride with the comet as it passes around the Sun!

She has written a number of steampunk short stories, children's science-learning books, and a full length elfpunk novel. She is also an avid tennis fan and has written for the *Bleacher Report* as claudia celestial girl. Red Phoenix Books, her publishing arm, established in 2002, has published the books of award-winning author, Carol Fenner, and debut author, Diane Schochet.

Other Stories by Claudia Alexander:

Landship Engine: Agincourt Over Again

The Vintner's Tale: An Adaptation of Shakespeare's The Winter's Tale

Windows to Adventure: Which of the Mountains is Greatest of All?

The Vintner's Tale appears as Leo's Mechanical Queen in the Steampunk Shakespeare anthology, *The Omnibus of Dr. Bill Shakes and the Magnificent Ionic Pentatetrameter*

ABOUT ANGIOLETTA CORADINI

The character of Angie in *Windows to Adventure* was named after **Dr. Angioletta Coradini**. Dr. Coradini, from Italy, was one of the most important women to ever study the space sciences. Over the course of her life, she used both instruments and computers to study and compare planets, the Earth, and the nebula from which planets form.

Of all the instruments she built, one was a key instrument for exploring planet Venus. The instrument was on the VEX Mission (Venus Express). Its name was VIRTIS, which stands for Visible and Infrared Thermal Imaging Spectrometer.

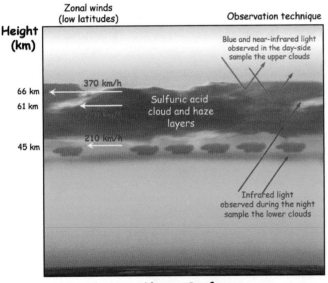

Venus Surface

This picture is one that was created by the VIRTIS instrument. It measured the heat coming from various cloud levels of Venus, helped determine where the clouds were found, how fast the wind speed's were, and the location of the top edge of Venus's troposphere.

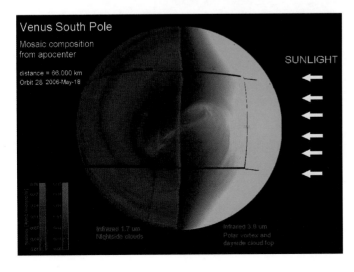

This picture shows a special cloud formation (unique to Venus) at Venus's south pole. Dr. Coradini's instrument, VIRTIS, discovered this feature by making measurements in infrared light.

PHOTO CREDITS

More Windows to Adventure

Windows to Adventure, Book 1 / Which of the Mountains is Greatest of All?
While exploring, Angie and Rashad discover a magical creature calling itself "AboGado." When AboGado volunteers to take them places, Rashad readily agrees, while Angie worries about the risks. AboGado takes them to visit the greatest of the solar system's mountains, including ancient Denali, beautiful Mt Fuji, youthful Mauna Kea, Olympus Mons (Mars), Maxwell Montes (Venus), and Rheasilvia (asteroid Vesta). Each of the mountains vociferously makes their case for being the greatest. Upon their safe return, Angie assumes custody of the magical creature.
ISBN-13: 978-0-9726290-2-7

Windows to Adventure, Book 3 / How High Up is That?
Angie, Rashad, De De, and Julio wonder what is higher in the sky than the airplanes. To make the magic of AboGado work, all they need to do is ask the question! AboGado introduces them to Sky and the atmospheric family. They step through the window and Sky takes them on a tour of the atmosphere and beyond.
ISBN-13: 978-0-9726290-4-1

Windows to Adventure, Book 4 / Keeping Warmth in a Bag
The AboGado tells a story of Badger, Fox, and Moose, who rescued summer from Bear's house. It is true that winter can stay too long and summer never comes, but it doesn't make sense. Sky comes to explain why the climate sometimes changes.
ISBN-13: 978-0-9726290-5-8

Windows to Adventure, Book 5 / Why must Winter Come?
It is a blustery day with sprinkles of snow. Angie's mother wants the kids to come inside and play. The kids ask the AboGado why must winter come. Troposphere, part of the atmospheric family, comes to talk about the great storms he can make.
ISBN-13: 978-1-9377819-5-8

Windows to Adventure, Book 6 / A Star's Life
Rashad's friend Julio has always been curiously drawn to the topic of black holes. Yi Mei has always felt drawn to this group of friends. AboGado brings forth Amaterasu, the Japanese goddess of the Sun, to take Rashad, Julio, Angie, De De, and new friend Yi Mei, on a journey to meet Amaterasu's friends among the stars. Along the way they meet very young stars, very old stars, and a finally, at the end of a star's life, a black hole.
ISBN-13: 978-0-9726290-6-5

Windows to Adventure, Book 7 / Extraterrestrial Life
Yi Mei is having a difficult time fitting in. When she asks about living and adapting, AboGado introduces three stars. Each one describes, the extreme environment near their planets, and how living beings would have to adapt. The kids each imagine a type of life that could survive, and Julio makes a fateful wish that the aliens they've imagined might come to life. Because of the magic of AboGado, the imagined aliens do come to

life. To escape from the book, the extraterrestrials must work together to survive in the alien world of today's Earth.
ISBN-13: 978-0-9726290-7-2

Windows to Adventure, Book 8 / The Many Faces of Earth

Almost all the kids are at Angie's house. They decide that they want to see the spirit of Earth. Soon the Earth appears in the AboGado, and off they go, around the world, to see what Earth looks like.
ISBN-13: 978-1-9377819-1-0

Windows to Adventure, Book 9 / Jupiter and the Fastest Wind

Though the biggest planet of all, Jupiter seems sensitive about comparing itself with other planets. Jupiter explains its position as "The Broken Morning Star," a comparison with Venus, before taking Angie and Rashad through the AboGado's portal to experience the bumpy, chaotic, & rapidly moving roller coaster of the Jupiter troposphere. Along the way, a race evolves to compare the atmospheric winds of the many planets, moons, and even stars.
ISBN-13: 978-1-9377819-0-3

Windows to Adventure, Book 10 / The Sun, Our Star

Yi Mei wears colorful clothing. This conflicts with tradition in Yi Mei's family, making her uncomfortable and unsure of herself. Angie and Yi Mei ask AboGado to take them to the Sun, but the Sun is busy. The Innuit goddess of the Sun, Seqinek, guides them on a tour of the Sun's "work," its struggle to hold its body together, the rainbow of light it's capable of creating, and the wind that it constantly blows. This book has an artistic contribution and foreword from Astronaut Alan Bean.
ISBN-13: 978-1-9377819-91-0

Windows to Adventure, Book 11 / Galileo Galilei

The AboGado tells the kids why the spirits admire humans. Demeter volunteers to take the kids backward in time to witness the trial of Galileo Galilei, a scientist who stood up for his beliefs and got in trouble. The kids get to wear fancy clothes, and experience the 16th century. Will the kids have the courage of Galileo when they get into trouble? The aliens from Book 7 try to go backward in time with them.
ISBN-13: 978-1-9377819-2-7

Windows to Adventure, Book 12 / The Milky Way Galaxy and the Path of Awe

De De has always wanted to know about galaxies and why they twist and spiral. Sky takes De De, Angie, and the rest on a tour of galaxies, including what we see when we look at the Milky Way. Sky shows how the Milky Way, a clustered band of stars, creates a *Path of Awe* across the night sky. When a Deer and an Antelope appear in AboGado's portal, the kids find themselves on a wild race across the great path created by the Milky Way, as Deer and Antelope compete for the right to roam the range.
ISBN-13: 978-1-9377819-3-4

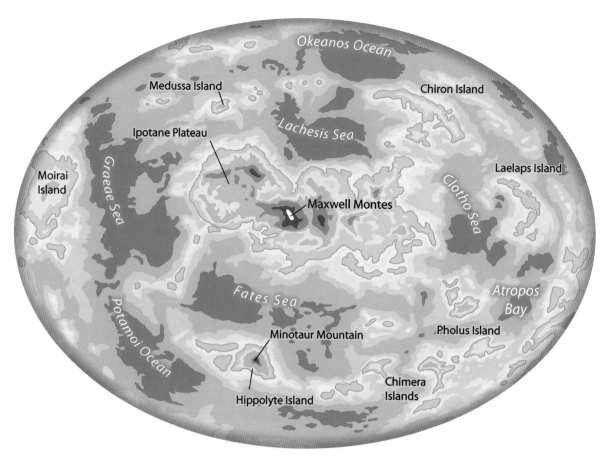

A Fantasy Venus

Made in the USA
San Bernardino, CA
11 August 2014